The Circle Book

Jenny Mosley

Positive Press

Published by Positive Press Ltd
28A Gloucester Road
Trowbridge
Wiltshire
BA14 0AA
England

Originally published 1992, in photocopied format
with yellow card covers and tape binding

New edition under Positive Press imprint 2001
Reprinted 2007

© Jenny Mosley

ISBN 9780953012251

The 'essence' of Circle Time

❑ Circle Time is a pleasant, comfortable time when the class comes together for reflection, enjoyment and celebration. Problems can be discussed openly and solved with the participation of the whole group. The emphasis is on help and not blame.

❑ The children and staff are seated comfortably, in a circle, so that everyone can be seen by everyone else.

❑ The group can focus on achievements either as a whole or by individuals. Praise and rewards can be handed out by any members of the group.

❑ Skills of listening, looking and thinking are highlighted in circle games.

❑ Topics for discussion and comment can cover anything, e.g. school work, classroom behaviour and rules, dinner time, playtime, travelling to and from school, interests at home, news, world events, worries and successes. Discussion is controlled, which makes it difficult for children to merely complain or tell tales. The onus is put on individuals to solve problems rather than just voice them. Children learn to recognise anti-social behaviour and its effect on others. No child may mention any individual (child, parent, teacher) in a negative way. They are taught to say 'Someone is ...', 'Some people are ...' – in this way people's reputations are safeguarded.

❑ Circle work must have structure, i.e. a preface, one game and/or round, one open discussion, one celebratory activity, and a calming ritual to end.

❑ Circle work needs to be regular to be effective; the more frequently it takes place the more the children will speak out and air their views. Circle Time is about giving responsibility to children and should take place at least once a week, but ideally every day.

A model for building an effective and happy school

A framework to show how Quality Circle Time develops a whole school policy on self-esteem and positive behaviour

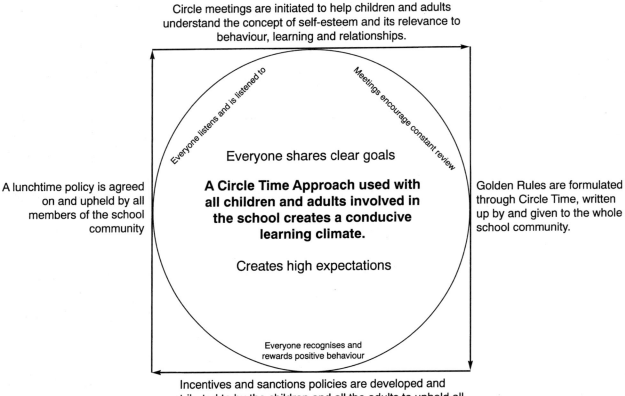

Circle meetings are initiated to help children and adults understand the concept of self-esteem and its relevance to behaviour, learning and relationships.

Everyone listens and is listened to

Meetings encourage constant review

Everyone shares clear goals

A Circle Time Approach used with all children and adults involved in the school creates a conducive learning climate.

Creates high expectations

A lunchtime policy is agreed on and upheld by all members of the school community

Golden Rules are formulated through Circle Time, written up by and given to the whole school community.

Everyone recognises and rewards positive behaviour

Incentives and sanctions policies are developed and contributed to by the children and all the adults to uphold all the positive behaviours outlined in the Golden Rules. All adults and children are encouraged to use these policies equally.

Ground rules for circle work

A good idea is to do one or two *initial* circle sessions which include enjoyable games, then work out ground rules *with* the whole group. This ensures the group is more motivated towards the idea of Circle Time and therefore is prepared to negotiate and commit itself to these rules.

If the group doesn't suggest some of the following rules itself, you propose them. One way of really finding out what individuals think is to ask them to *vote* on suggestions by *closing their eyes* and raising hands; (this stops peer group pressure).

Proposed rules

❑ Everyone has a turn to speak; (use sentence-completion 'rounds', e.g. 'I feel fed up when ...'). You take your turn and don't make it longer than the others. Share *your* feelings as genuinely and honestly as possible.

Initially a pupil can say 'Pass', but the topic will be given back to him/her at the end of the round; (by then they usually have ideas).

❑ If a round contains some dilemmas or problems that *you* think affect the whole group, *consult with them* to see if they would like to discuss these further. Then open the discussion to all: you will often find that pupils who've been involved in the initial round will be far more prepared to speak.

Don't ever assume that *you* know what the group wants to follow up. Always *check with them* to see if they are interested in certain topics; sometimes discussion doesn't develop as you expect because basically pupils aren't interested!

❑ Whenever anyone speaks, their views must be listened to and their contributions, however 'way out', must be treated with respect.

❑ No 'put-downs' or negative comments about pupils' contributions are tolerated.

❑ Any child who does not behave appropriately during Circle Time is given a verbal or – for younger children – a visual (sad face) warning. If they continue to misbehave, they must sit outside the circle and not participate in the activities for a set period of time. Remember, though, to remove the visual warning as soon as the child responds.

❑ For groups unused to circle work and during rounds, the 'conch strategy' is used: a child is allowed to talk only whenever they hold the 'talking object'. This can be a small teddy or a painted wooden egg. As they become more skilled at listening, the 'conch' is used only for the rounds.

❑ All children should agree that anything mentioned in the circle is meant only for that circle. They must not gossip outside. If this does happen, discuss the issue with the whole group – but encourage *forgiveness* at all times.

❑ When personal and controversial issues are under discussion, **warn** students only to say as much as they feel is 'safe', i.e. be very sure, from the beginning, to tell them that only *they* are 'in charge' of the information they entrust to the whole group. They must realise that, although confidentiality is encouraged, it is not guaranteed. Therefore, if there's anything too personal or private which they feel they need to discuss further, suggest to them that they ask to see you for a private chat at a different time. Perhaps offer to be available one break-time a week.

Points to remember

Don't overdo Circle Time: making it over-long will kill interest.

Keep it pacey. Make sure you vary the circle approach. It includes warm-ups, games, paired talking/listening exercises, rounds, discussion and roles.

Evaluate regularly, e.g. 'The most boring/interesting part for me was ...'

Make sure you follow up any injustices or things that are 'going wrong' for students. Circle Time *must not* exist in isolation. They will learn to trust you only if they perceive you as genuinely caring about their needs and being prepared to *do* something on their behalf.

Make sure *you* always take a few minutes to evaluate the session too. If possible, set up some form of support with colleagues to discuss the issues that are raised.

N.B. Try to make sure that you include some fun – always end on a light-hearted note, with a 'fun' activity followed by a calming exercise so the children are 'returned' to the next activity feeling 'lighter'.

Starter ideas for Circle Time activities

Remind children to use their thinking, looking, listening, speaking and concentrating skills. More ideas will be found on pages 28-36.

1. Examples of rounds
I get fed up when ...
I am afraid of ...
I feel happy when ...
Something I have learnt today ...
I was pleased with myself because ...
I was kind when ...
I like it when ...
I don't like it when ... *This can lead on to* 'Does anyone need some help?'

2. My hobby is ...

Children volunteer to mime a hobby that they enjoy, for the others to guess. *This can lead on to* discussion of hobbies in general and why they are good for us.

3. Silent Circle

A noisy object, e.g. tambourine, bunch of keys, is passed around the circle trying to avoid any sound being made. *This can lead on to* 'I like silence because ...'

4. What is special about you?

One child leaves the circle and waits outside the classroom. The remaining children tell the teacher everything that is special about the absent child, e.g. she has a good sense of humour, she has lovely brown hair, she is kind. The teacher writes down all the comments on a sheet of paper. The absent child, while she is out of the classroom, can also write or draw pictures about why her class team are special. *This can lead on to* discussion and appreciation of each individual's uniqueness and the realisation that everyone has some special gifts.

5. Acting Headteachers – the drama strategy 'Mantle of the Expert'

The children are told they are headteachers of brilliant schools. A few props would be useful, e.g. glasses, briefcase, folder. The teacher uses a 'microphone' to announce 'We have brought you here today because the BBC has learnt that you have wonderful ideas on how to make children and teachers happy in your schools.' The children are invited to take turns in describing the ideas they have implemented in their schools to make life happy and enjoyable. *This can lead on to* discussion of strategies, e.g. Golden Rules, behaviour targets.

6. Pass it on

The children pass 'body parts', e.g. elbow, toes, knee, around the circle. This is done by making contact with the child on your left, touching body part to body part, i.e. elbow to elbow, knee to knee. Finally, the children pass a smile. This activity needs to be prefaced by reminding children of the Golden Rule of *Do be gentle* and praise should be given for really calm body contact. Afterwards you can discuss how we feel when people play safely and keep to the rules.

Circle Time can contribute to the National Curriculum

Reading the following excerpts from National Curriculum documentation, it is obvious that the circle strategies of listening and talking can help children reach attainment targets for English

'Children's first approach to language is through listening and talking. Talk is often the first record of any individual or group in response to events and preparation for action. It is our prime means of communication and it is proper that its importance should be recognised in the curriculum in schools.

'The effectiveness of talking and listening is determined not only by the ability to use speech appropriately, but also by the ability to listen. The former includes being able to adjust ways of speaking – such as tone and vocabulary – according to audience, context and purpose; the latter includes skills of concentration, assimilation and timing. The use and interpretation of silence is also an important factor.

> "I think that we communicate only too well in our silence, in what is unsaid ..." – **Harold Pinter**

'Development of oral skills will involve increased sensitivity to the nuances of language and presentation, and to the implications of context. We would expect pupils to demonstrate their growing competence as both speakers and listeners by:

* developing increasing accuracy and precision in describing experience, expressing opinions and articulating personal feelings;
* demonstrating an increasing ability to evaluate and to reflect;
* showing an increasing ability to function collaboratively, e.g. involving others in a discussion, listening to and giving weight to the opinions of others, perceiving the relevance of contributions, timing contributions, adjusting and adapting to feedback.'

What teachers have written about the benefits of Circle Time

I think this approach has enormous value in helping create a positive atmosphere. This makes for a more effective and successful school.

It gives all children a chance to participate on an equal footing with both their peers and the teacher and raises their self-esteem when they realise that everyone's ideas are valid.

I think these activities help to get the class together and to bring out into the open social problems that may exist

I feel it gives children a better understanding of each other and of us as adults.

It is practical, constructive, effective – confidence boosting

It develops patience, boosts confidence, develops self-esteem.

Encourages children to put others before themselves.

A feeling of togetherness and self-esteem is promoted – everybody's views and opinions are valued and investigated. The quiet, controlled atmosphere helps to make it a special event.

Builds up self-confidence and self-esteem. Creates a group feeling. Encourages a responsible attitude to the group's behaviour. Makes individuals aware of others' feelings and needs.

Encourages the children to be self-controlled and to think of others in the class.

Making individuals aware of each other's needs and thoughts. Encouraging children to take turns and develop the skill of listening

Active learning, opportunity to explore feelings, socially acceptable behaviour and other issues against a backdrop of fun activities. Opportunity for peer pressure to alter and adapt behaviour.

For the pupils the benefits include a 'group' feeling, increased self-esteem, greater sensitivity, more confident use of language and, above all, a more positive approach to life.

For the teacher benefits include a sounder knowledge of the class, a greater trust in the capabilities of the children, a wider knowledge of himself through the children, and an opportunity for fun.

Creating a feeling of belonging to a group and then feeling secure within that group. Of feeling then that your opinions have value – are being listened to. That each individual has the power to change things.

It is an ideal opportunity to build on relationships – you have time as a teacher to concentrate solely on this and on listening to children. Good relationships between child and child, child and teacher and between child and midday supervisor or welfare assistant are vital. You can also concentrate on boosting self-esteem and ensure all have a turn.

Children understand that no one is perfect and that we are Still fond of people even if they sometimes do things that are unkind.

Quality Circle Time gets results

The following report is from a teacher whose school initiated a Quality Circle Time programme.

After teaching a class for 18 months, I was asked to introduce a new development to them called Circle Time.

The formalised approach to 'circling' was a dream to implement. The children loved it! Every aspect – the focus of specific skills development, the games, the chats, the protection of anonymity – were all readily accepted and internalised.

The children also decided to introduce the other children in the school and their parents to Circle Time by means of a school service. Their enthusiasm for and enjoyment of Circle Time was readily transmitted to the rest of the school. Some parents expressed disbelief at the ability of their children to confront difficult situations and to deal with them in such a mature manner. Many parents felt that Circle Time offered strategies for dealing with problems that they could find useful in their homes.

More confirmation of the effectiveness of Circle Time comes from *A Study of the Effectiveness of Circle Time in Raising Self-Esteem and Promoting Positive Behaviour* by Jan Marshall (unpublished dissertation 1995), from which the following extracts have been taken.

The most obvious impression gained is the fact that the children responded so positively to Circle Time. The whole group responded to the structure of the sessions ... as if this was one part of their lives where the pattern of the session itself gave them a much needed security.

Those children whose self-esteem had been identified as being quite low were the ones who cited 'passing a smile' as their favourite activity ... maybe this was because they weren't on the receiving end of many smiles normally. Even carrying out a progressive rhyme like 'heads, shoulders, knees and toes' with a class normally so lacking in self-discipline, within the confines of the circle was carried out sensibly and steadily.

The point of this project was to use a range of tools to evaluate the impact of Circle Time on children's self-esteem and behaviour. It would seem that the data obtained and analysed unmistakably point towards a change ... towards more positive behaviour.

Circle Time has an important part to play in the life of any school. The effect of spending as little as 30 minutes per week in structured Circle Time sessions is likely to reap many benefits in terms of pupil behaviour and promoting a positive school ethos ... For an increasing number of children in our schools Circle Time may be the only opportunity they have to experience such a consistently secure and caring atmosphere.

The circle approach helps children to solve their own problems with learning and relationships.

I think circle time is good because it helps you with your problems like when you fall out with your freinds the next minuite your playing it sorts out really any problem I think that every school should have them. When people are being bullyed it usellay helps then. I like haveing circle meetings I think they are good for all diffrent kinds of things I think they are really good. ideas.

Circle work enhances self-esteem

This paper was written by a young teacher who had recently attended a Circle Time course and decided to introduce it into his own class. He comments on the results:

Spring Term

I think that Circle Time has been a really successful and useful activity. It has been enjoyable and educational for both the children and myself.

At first the children found it quite difficult to cope with sitting still for 40 minutes or so, but from the very start they were able to respond not only to the game playing but also to the listening and talking activities. The quality of their contributions has noticeably improved. They have become more direct, more personal and much clearer. Some of the children who participate the most now were the ones who found it most difficult to express their feelings when we first started.

In a short time there have been noticeable changes in the children's attitudes and behaviour. They still fall out, fight etc, but they are more aware of how unsatisfactory this state of affairs is, and seem to be more equipped to deal with these situations and resolve them. A much more caring attitude exists between the children, a feeling that our class is special and that they belong to it. The 'Thinking' dialogue books have made it easier for them to approach me with worries and problems.

The children look forward to the sessions and take them seriously. In fact a colleague and myself were quite surprised at their level of awareness as to the function of the circle, when we asked them to tell us what they liked about it at the end of last week's session. When we have missed a session I have noticed that there are more arguments, and agreements made not to call people names etc are broken. It is something that needs to be done on a regular basis.

We have not had the chance to really develop Circle Time, but have seen that it has great potential. Next term I think we could target individual children's needs and problems and get the whole class to work towards solutions. I think that this kind of approach could cause children to change behaviour if they realise that the whole class find it unacceptable, not just the teacher! It's worth a try! A system of rewards for children who achieve targets set by the children themselves is also a possible way forward. If this is seen by the children as a way of helping each other then it will really work.

As a case study, here are the weekly Circle Time sessions initiated by the young teacher. All of the activities listed are detailed at the end of this section.

Week 1

Opening game: Fruit Salad
                 – for fun, to mix people up

Circle: 'I like my next door neighbour because ...'
                 'I like myself because ...'
                 'I am good at ...'
                 – encourage positive statements about self and others

Closing game: The Sleeping Spell
                 – encourage eye contact, careful observation, fun

Follow up: Draw yourself on top half of paper
                 Write 'I like ... because' on sticky paper, using names of any of the other children
                 Stick on to the appropriate picture (limit of four per picture)

EVALUATION: Good response from children. Most very forthcoming. Brett found it difficult to respond. 'I like myself because' was sometimes shallow, in that the answers were 'because I'm pretty', 'because others like me'. Sandy could not answer 'I like myself' but dealt with the situation very well. They loved both games. Circle rules were learnt and reinforced. Talked about Think books – I think we will need to talk more so that they get more idea. No time for follow-up.

Week 2

Opening game: Fruit Salad – different leaders

Circle: 'The best thing someone has said about me ...'
                 'The worst thing someone has said about me ...'
                 Warm Fuzzy, Cold Prickly
                 – try to use 'warm fuzzy' statements for rest of day.

Closing game: The Sleeping Spell

EVALUATION: Children had remembered the 'rules' of the circle. Enjoyed warm-up game. Much harder questions – a few could not respond. Brainstormed 'warm fuzzy', 'cold prickly' and made notices of them. All agreed we liked 'warm fuzzy' best.. Linked hands in circle and made contract with one another to say 'warm fuzzies' from now on.

Week 3

Opening game: Carrot, Cabbage, Coleslaw (Vegetables, played as Fruit Salad)

Circle: Brainstorm different feelings
                  Make cards: 'happy', 'shy' etc
                  Put into Green class's Feeling Box
                  Take some out and do rounds
                  Ask about Warm Fuzzy, Cold Prickly
                  Ask if anyone has said anything they have regretted
                  How have they managed in playground?

Closing game: Pass a squeeze.

EVALUATION: Everyone had tried to use 'warm fuzzy' statements about each
                  other. Many had failed. Talked through 'cold prickly' things
                  that had been said. Identified playground main source.
                  Reinforced idea that Green class should use 'warm fuzzies'
                  and try and influence others.

                  Introduced Feelings Box. Brainstorm came up with 'happy',
                  sad', 'frustrated', 'nervous' feelings. Used 'sad' and
                  'frustrated'. Introduced empathy but it stopped the flow of the
                  circle (re-think). Some very revealing comments made –
                  John's 'I felt sad when my Dad left'.

                  Without my ever saying that they could, children who can't
                  cope are saying 'Pass it on' (Sandy, Janice). They seem
                  happy and comfortable in circle so allow it. Tried 'Pass a
                  squeeze' to finish – took a long time to catch on to it. This
                  session lasted 1 hour and was too long.

Week 4

Opening game: Apples, Peaches, Pears (Fruit Salad)
                  Practise Warm Fuzzy
                  'I like ... because'
                  Brainstorm

Circle: Mr Bish wants to make a star chart but instead of giving stars
                  for good work he wants you to think of things he should give
                  stars for.

                  Is there something special you would like Mr Bish to look for in
                  you, something you find difficult?

                  Explain 5 stars will mean a 5-star badge. A special award will
                  be a certificate.

Closing game:	Pass a squeeze.
EVALUATION:	Started well but group seemed rather restless. Made 'warm fuzzy' statements about each other. Anything they would like to change? Basically they did not understand what I meant. Made a mistake by not starting with myself – to set the tone. Became 'I would rather be called Luke than Gary', so decided to pick up on name-calling. Asked if they were called names they didn't like. Matthew was called 'goggle eyes' or 'four-eyes' because of his glasses, Brett was called 'spotted dick'. Made contract with class not to use those names and to tell Mr Bish if anyone did.
	Close with a very enthusiastic game of The Sleeping Spell.
	Paul and I agreed that we ought to be in circle twice a week. It is difficult having a set time – would prefer a spontaneous time when problems could be aired.
	N.B. Playground problems.

Week 5

Opening game:	England, Scotland, Ireland, Wales (Great Britain – played as Fruit Salad)
Circle:	Name calling. Ask Matthew and Brett if it has stopped.
	'I have a good time in the playground when ...' 'I had a bad time in the playground when ...' 'We have fun in the playground when ...' 'We have a bad time in the playground when ...' Brainstorm Contract with each other for good behaviour in the playground.
Closing game:	Retrieve the Keys
EVALUATION:	Excellent session today. Children very responsive and eager for circle time. Matthew and Brett both reported that they had not been called names. Explored playground behaviour. They are going to care for each other in the playground.

These are the circle activities used by the teacher in the previous case study:

Fruit Salad

The children are alternately named orange and apple around the circle. When you call out the name of a fruit, e.g. 'Apple', all the children in that category change seats. If you call 'Fruit Salad', all children change. You can increase the number of fruits depending on the age and competency of the children.

The Sleeping Spell

The children sit in a circle. A child is chosen to be the detective and leaves the room. Another child is chosen to be the magician, and the detective returns to stand in the centre of the circle. Without being seen by the detective, the magician winks at any child, who then 'falls asleep'. This continues until the detective correctly identifies the magician. Different children are then chosen to play the roles.

Warm Fuzzies and Cold Pricklies

Explain to the children that 'warm fuzzy' statements make them or other people feel good about themselves, i.e. they are positive; e.g. 'I am good at colouring' or 'You were very helpful'. 'Cold pricklies' are negative or unkind statements that hurt people's feelings or make you feel bad about yourself; e.g. 'You've got big ears' or 'I'm hopeless at maths'. Let the children offer some examples.

Pass a Squeeze

The children hold hands around the circle. Squeeze the hand of the child on your left and tell him to pass the squeeze on to the child on his left. The squeeze is passed from child to child around the circle until it comes back to you. Tell the children that they must only give a gentle squeeze.

Retrieve the keys

A bunch of keys is placed on the ground in the centre of the circle. The children close their eyes. Choose a child to retrieve the keys by walking around the outside of the circle and tapping the child on the shoulder. This child must attempt to enter the circle, pick up the keys and return to her seat without being heard by the other children.

A Ring of Confidence

(*Quotes taken from a feature article by Susannah Kirkman in the Times Educational Supplement for 12 October 1990.*)

Discipline has improved and pupils' self-esteem risen since 'circle work' was introduced in Wiltshire primaries.

... recalling and sharing past humiliations helps teachers to put themselves in their pupils' shoes.

The Elton Report showed that injustice still plays a big part in our schools and that some teachers are still punishing by humiliating pupils. It also commented on the lack of praise and rewards for good behaviour.

Everyone from dinner ladies to parents and pupils is involved in making the rules.

'I feel it's not my values I'm imposing now, but our values', said Peter Gerrish, head of Avenue School in Warminster.

Adults' and children's ideas were virtually identical.

Withdrawing privileges is seen as the most effective sanction.

Far from feeling intimidated by the frank nature of circle work, the pupils seem to enjoy it.

The children are very honest about their own behaviour problems because they want help.

Their unacceptable behaviour is a burden to them.

The children are more co-operative and friendlier to me and each other (since introducing circle time sessions).

Circle work has increased children's articulacy and self-confidence.

Teachers emphasised that the philosophy would not work unless all the staff were involved.

'I've been a dinner lady for almost 19 years and I feel more involved with the staff than ever before.'

... the emphasis on self-esteem reinforces the school's caring ethos and makes it a popular choice for parents.

Wiltshire is delighted with the success of the project, which it sees as a unique response to the Elton Report.

More case studies

The following report is from a headteacher whose school initiated the circle programme for children and dinner ladies with consultancy support.

There were severe problems between our children's behaviour at lunchtimes and the expectations of our MDSAs. We also had some conflict between some of the older children in the top year. One child had very low self-esteem and constantly provoked others within his peer group.

The consultant worked with two classes in the morning, finding out the problems that the children felt were important to them. They discussed 'golden rules' that would be displayed within their room and sanctions if the rules were broken.

The lunchtime session with the dinner ladies was I felt most helpful. The feedback from the MDSAs to the consultant was of great importance to me in revealing where the ladies were finding stress and how we could make their job better and give their self-esteem a boost. I believe it was easier for them to talk to an 'outsider'.

In the short time available the consultant worked very hard and her results were amazing. She helped to plan a reward system for the whole school to use ensuring that the MDSAs had an essential part to play in the fulfilment of the scheme.

Since implementing the scheme the lunchtimes have improved beyond recognition; this is not an exaggeration – the ladies are happier and the children working more together. There are confrontations but nothing like the first part of the year.

We all feel that the consultancy was wonderful but not enough as time was limited. The staff meetings held after school again were not long enough, as everything had to be done in 'double time' to fit in. All of my staff would appreciate at least another meeting at the school to see how we have progressed and where to go from here. Also the teaching staff need their self-esteem helped at a time when we seem to have no time to achieve satisfaction in our chosen job. The consultant gave us a feeling of worth and cared for our feelings.

The following programme of circle sessions was developed as part of a research study

Active Groupwork: A short programme of circle activities selected to encourage the group to interact with each other, to foster group co-operation, to boost self-confidence of its individual members and to help create the right climate for the group to progress to their own negotiated problem-solving activities, which will eventually require less leader direction. It is important that the leader makes explicit the reasons *why* certain activities have been chosen and consults with the group as to their 'effectiveness'.

Form a circle with chairs. A circle is chosen to emphasise unity, ensure eye-contact for all members and help create a 'safe' boundary: all physical and verbal activity will take place within its space. The leader agrees to join in all activities as a ordinary member of the group.

Session 1

1. Fruit Salad

   Players sit in circle on chairs, one player in middle. Player in middle names players in circle alternately 'Apple' or 'Orange'. If he then calls ORANGE all Oranges change places. If he calls APPLE all Apples change places. If he calls FRUIT SALAD all players change places. The player in the middle tries to sit on a chair, and the player left without a chair goes into the middle.

   This activity is chosen to encourage students to mix with others and to ensure that, when the leader stops the activity, all students are thoroughly mixed – this has been achieved in an atmosphere of fun and eliminated any possible 'aggro'!

2. Each member introduces him/herself and physically makes one action to indicate how they are feeling *now*, e.g. John is tired – stretches, Helen is excited – stamps feet. The whole group imitates that person's chosen contribution. This causes laughter and encourages participants to know each other's names and feelings in an informal atmosphere.

3. The children and leader 'mill' inside the circle – they have two minutes to shake each other's hands, give their names and tell a funny fact about themselves.

4. The children return to their circle seats and each person stands and introduces another – 'This is John, he likes jam and cucumber sandwiches.' John then introduces another person until the whole circle is standing.

5. A child is asked to walk around labelling each child A-B-A-B around the circle. All the As move their chairs to face the Bs: thus an inner and outer circle is formed. In these pairs discover three things you have in common that you like, and three things that you both dislike.

6. Re-form the larger circle. The As introduce their B partners and recount the things they both dislike. The Bs then introduce their A partners and recount the things they both like.

   The aim is to introduce the concept of shared experiences and individual differences at a very basic level.

I think circle time is Good because it stops you Fighting. and it helps you a Lot about your Problems and sometimes it gets you out of troble. by Timothy

Session 2

1. Within circle: How many knees can you touch in one minute?
                       How many elbows can you touch in one minute?

   Rather than greet each other with a 'normal' handshake, you have to say hello in an unusual way – e.g. back to back shaking hands, rubbing knees, etc. (Because touch is introduced in the framework of a game, it is achieved easily in an atmosphere of fun.)

2. Re-form large circle. Each member *jumps* in saying his/her name with a chosen gesture; everyone copies each time. However small or extravagant a gesture is chosen, this activity emphasises the equal contribution and impact of each child to the group.

3. In the circle, each member addresses another person with an 'interesting' question, e.g. 'John, could you tell me about your favourite TV programme please?'

4. Each person writes on a sticky label their name and an activity they really enjoy. They then put the label on their chest. The children mill around within the circle to see how many people they can meet in two minutes and find out about their chosen activity. They repeat this action but the task is to see how *long* they can talk to one person about their activity without having to move away.

5. Re-form circle. A 'round' discussion is held, focusing on how it felt rushing around collecting 'info' and how it felt when members asked questions and then stayed to listen to the answers. Then each child introduces one other child from the circle with the activity that they are interested in; that same child is then invited either to tell the group more or other members can ask further questions if they so wish. Eventually each child will have contributed.

I think that circle meetings are good.
Because they can help solv some
problems. It can also be a lot of
fun.

I Think circle meetings are important
because it makes us all quiet

Session 3

1. Explain that the following introductory game is being used for two reasons: that it serves a purpose of reminding us of the good feelings we get when we are part of a group having fun and the bad feelings we may get when we feel left out or different. Ask for a volunteer, explaining it is a difficult one. (Choose a popular member of the form.) He/she stands in the middle and the rest of the group move clockwise, covering the seats with their bottoms as they move around. (Therefore there is always an empty chair but it appears/disappears as the group circle moves around.) The volunteer's task is to try and sit on an empty chair, but as he/she dashes towards it the circle, as if with one 'mind', goes into action. As the game progresses, the moving group experiences great hilarity as a result of the movement and the success of thwarting the increasingly determined, wildly-dashing, volunteer.

2. After the above game is finished, the volunteer sits in the middle of the circle and members are asked if any of them can identify how the volunteer may be feeling. This is achieved by individuals coming forward and putting a hand on the shoulder of the volunteer and speaking aloud their thoughts – e.g. 'I am feeling very stupid ... everyone else was having a good time.' Ideas are close to his/her feelings. Should the theme of 'rejection' not surface, the teacher comments on how the scene looked to her as an outsider, and how it is reminiscent of similar playground scenes and the feeling it personally evokes for her.

3. In a 'round', each child completes a sentence: 'A time when I felt left out was ...' or 'Some people feel left out when ...' – whichever they choose. (The shyer ones are able to choose the less threatening alternative.)

4. Brainstorm all the things we as individuals can do to help others who sometimes are 'left out'.

5. Usually in a brainstorm evolving from the above activity, students mention 'being kind', 'talking to others': the teacher's task is then briefly to wind up the session by counselling on the meaning of empathy and the power of individuals to make others happy.

Session 4

1. Circle: A round of 'something I have done in the past that made someone happier', e.g. 'I let my sister use my computer'; (usually in such rounds the family predominates.)

2. Explain you would like to expand this idea re their classmates. In pairs pinpoint three things they look for in a friend.

3. Re-form the circle; ask each pair to tell their ideas.

4. The teacher initiates a conversation about the fact that all individuals have something to contribute. 'As this is the penultimate session and all members have been so co-operative and sensible ... it is now the right time for me to know a little more about you all, and to trust you to do the next activity.' Explain the forthcoming activity in no. 5 (below) and the importance of really thinking hard about positive remarks, as these can often help how a person feels about themselves. Brainstorm good remarks we can say in general about our classmates (giving no names) and analyse jointly which ones are really positive and which ones don't really qualify.

5. The teacher walks around the outside of the circle putting both hands on the shoulders of each child, and asks any member of the group to mention something positive about that person. (Contributions will range – despite earlier exercise – from 'John, I've noticed you are very generous' to 'Mary, I like the shoes you wore the other day.') It is important to allow only one contribution for each child, as the popular members could receive more and thus lower the confidence of the others. If, as suggested above, the quality of the contributions varies, it is important that the teacher expands the 'weaker' ones in a positive way, e.g. 'Yes, Mary, I noticed your shoes and the way you always take care with your appearance and keep things tidy.'

6. Tell the children that you have heard and noticed many positive things about all individuals. Ask them to listen to the following list and mentally tick the statements that apply to them.

> 'I try and listen when people talk'
> 'I like a good laugh'
> 'I'm capable of helping someone who is upset'
> 'I have shared my toys or hobbies in the past'

(Make a long list with the prior help of the form and subject teachers to ensure that every child will be capable of silently agreeing to at least one item on the list.)

I think circle meetings are important because you can tork too eachther

Paula.

Circle time

I think circle time is good because you can talk about your problems at school   I think younger children and older children get bullied. I don't think people should get bullied and called names. They are beginning to become interesting every time we have one. And I think the Traffic Lights are good because you do not get disturbed and putting our hands up when the teacher puts hers up. The Do not disturb signs are good as well.

Session 5 Development of the previous session – letting the children take responsibility for circle activities

Explain that the preceding sessional activities had been selected to realise the areas discussed at the beginning. Now that a certain level of trust and co-operation has been reached it is possible to hand back the responsibility for deciding the issues and topics, and the ways of tackling them, to the group.

Brainstorm ideas: children write down topics which range from lessons, getting ready for exams, discipline and control to uniforms, worries, teachers and falling out with friends.

Explain that one way of arriving at a consensus is to ask the children to close their eyes whilst one person reads the list, and they choose one they want to vote for with their hands whilst another pupil counts; this lessens the chance of people being 'swayed'.

In this session, the majority of pupils vote to look at the theme of 'teachers', especially 'bad' teachers.

Explain we could do 'rounds' to share our ideas, or pair work, or we could use role-play. The children choose role-play.

Explain that as a professional, one has to remain ignorant of actual names, and ask them to respect this.

The children decide a 'typical' scene that can cause them anger and frustration: namely, being shouted at and disbelieved by a teacher demanding homework when a pupil's reason for not doing it is genuine, but he or she doesn't want to say it aloud in front of class as it is personal.

Some were disappointed that they couldn't play a part – the first two volunteers had been accepted – and I ask if they'd like me to suggest a way they could be further involved. They agree and I explain it is a method called 'doubling': as the action progresses, any member of the circle can go into the middle and put their hand on an actor's shoulder, 'freeze' the play and speak aloud their thoughts.

The scene is acted out in the middle of the circle. I start the doubling by putting my hand on the shoulder of a pupil and speaking my thoughts: 'I hope he doesn't start shouting too loudly, everyone's looking at me, I loathe loud-mouthed bullies.' Thereafter at least ten of the class got up and 'doubled'. Thoughts ranged from 'I've got to prove myself in front of these kids that I mean business' (for the teacher), to 'I have to put up with Mum and Dad arguing every morning and now him as well ... I hate school, nobody understands.' The scene ends with the pupil walking out whilst the teacher is in the middle of a tirade.

I ask if this is typical of certain frustrations. We do a round of 'Teachers make me fed up when ...' Lots of nods and agreements accompany the contributions.

We decide to focus on the immediate problem that has been acted out and brainstorm ways that the pupil could have avoided the whole situation. It was agreed that the most positive suggestions from the group involved the pupil forestalling any confrontation by attempting to apologise for lack of homework before the lesson started, so that the teacher isn't put on the spot; alternatively, going in the morning straight to one teacher they like and confiding to them; if confrontation couldn't be avoided it was best to lower the head and say as little as possible, as opposed to the more aggressive hands-in-pocket stance the actor adopted. (I say nothing in this discussion.)

Extract from a tape-recording of a discussion that took place after role-play:

A   Teachers can feel really terrible, can you see how the teacher feels really terrible?

B   Yes, it's not that she's exactly a different human being, she's the same as us.

A   Is she emotional?

B   Yes, Yes, – True.

A   We are all the same.

A   How do you feel so far about the teacher? – in the play we've just done, you spoke all the thoughts I felt.

B   I don't know – it's realising it – realising how you felt and realising how they feel. Putting yourself in their position.

circle meeting

I think circle meetings are inportant because you slove problems. And help people feal beter as they have been Fighting or hurt by people like if they have been naged.

25

Case studies continued: Report on Circle Time with years 5 and 6 by an Advisory Teacher for SEN (Thurrock)

In the spring of 1999, having been inspired by Jenny Mosley's work, I began to support a class of year 5 and year 6 children through circle time. As an advisory teacher for special educational needs, I had visited the class to advise on programmes for a child with cerebral palsy and a child with ADHD. The class had had a succession of supply teachers and the behaviour of some of the pupils had become challenging. However, an excellent Learning Support Assistant had been supporting the class and was providing the stability that the class needed.

Together we decided to maintain the circle time and build on the start that we had made earlier that year before the illness of the class teacher. Initially, circle time had been difficult: arguments and fights would develop over who should sit on which chair. A significant number of the class were unable to listen to each other during a speaking round. However, through games requiring listening (the pirate and the keys) and co-operation (passing a clap round the circle), the children began to enjoy circle time and to develop their skills.

Because the Learning Support Assistant had a qualification in drama, she was able to use her knowledge and experience to develop these skills further. One day, she spoke to me of her concerns regarding the child with cerebral palsy in the class: he was being laughed at by several of his classmates and was very unhappy. She was keen to address this during circle time. I was not so sure: I spoke of how difficult this might be for the particular child and, also, how Jenny Mosley advises that individuals are not named in a negative way. The Learning Support Assistant said she would talk to the child and see how he felt about it.

The next week, she reported that John had agreed to bring the matter up during circle time. They had decided on a signal: she would tell the story of the little lame boy left behind when all the other children had followed the Pied Piper. At a point in the story, she would look at John and he would indicate by nodding or shaking his head whether he wanted her to continue. So we went ahead. After the preface, the warm-up game and the opening round, the Learning Support Assistant began the story. She paused at the agreed point and John nodded. She then went on to tell the class that John wanted to speak to them all.

John held the speaking object and explained to the class about cerebral palsy and how it affected him: he told them how frustrating it was not to be able to play football well or run as fast as the rest of the class. He spoke about how bad it made him feel when others laughed at him. There was one incident that had really upset him: years ago, at a birthday party, he had had a fit and had felt embarrassed ever since because members of the class had seen it. At this point, some of the children began to respond spontaneously. Several said that they remembered the incident and how sorry they were that John had fits. Others said sorry to John for laughing at him during football. One child burst into tears. She had a rare skin condition that sometimes resulted in hospitalisation. As there were two of us involved in circle time, the Learning Support Assistant was able to leave the circle to sit and talk to her. I began a speaking round during which each child said what they wanted to John, apologising for laughing at him and empathising with his condition. One child, who had been sitting next to me listening attentively for at least 40 minutes, said that he knew how John felt because he had ADHD and could not sit still! By this time, another class was waiting outside the room for their circle time session. I was aware that the session should not end at this point: Jenny Mosley had spoken of the importance of the celebration round and the closing game to bring everyone down safely from the emotional vulnerability of the open forum. We went back to the classroom, quickly pushed back the tables and sat in a circle. I thanked everyone for their contributions and, particularly, John, for his bravery in telling us how he felt. We then played a few of their favourite games to bring circle time to a close.

This circle time session taught me several things:

That the circle has great emotional power;

That children of 10 and 11 are capable of expressing their feelings honestly and/or with deep empathy;

That children from a 'deprived' area, many of whose skills are below average, can develop this emotional learning within a short time span.

In particular, the circle time format provided a safe vehicle for powerful emotions to be expressed. Without the framework of the circle and the fact that two adults were present, the situation could have become overwhelming and difficult to manage. Within the framework, the session enabled relationships to be repaired and strengthened through the power of the circle.

Further examples of Circle Time activities

Over the last decade my training courses and books have developed and extended the practice of Circle Time and the ways in which it can be used to address a range of situations and problems. There follow some sample activities used in the Jenny Mosley Quality Circle Time Model, taken from my books. For details of how to obtain the books themselves and a range of associated resource material, turn to the Training and Resources section on page 39.

Examples from *All Round Success* (1991, revised 1998)

The Keeper of the Keys

Good for   Group co-operation.
Helping class to develop concentration and listening skills.
Encouraging children to think about what they want to achieve and what stops them.

What to do   Sitting in a circle, the children make up a story about treasure – what it is, where it is, who its guardian is, e.g. a pirate and his jewels, a magician and his spell book, a monster and his gold. The children then suggest some 'obstacles' that can be set up within the circle, e.g. upturned chairs, pieces of scrunched-up newspaper, with a chair in the centre for the guardian. The treasure (something that could be noisy like keys or bells) is placed under the guardian's chair.

The first guardian is then chosen, blindfolded and seated in the centre of the circle. The rest of the group has to maintain complete silence whilst the chosen 'treasure-seeker' tries to negotiate the obstacles – by climbing over or through them – in order to retrieve the treasure and get back to his/her seat without being 'caught'. It is the guardian's task to listen carefully and when he/she thinks they hear the seeker to point to where they heard the sound and say 'Stop' loudly at the same time. The seeker has to freeze, and if the pointed finger is in their direction they have to return to their seat. The guardian is allowed only four attempts at stopping any seeker. If the treasure-seeker gets the treasure they receive a cheer and clap from the group and may elect the new guardian. (The guardian is also congratulated and thanked.)

28

Development   When children have become familiar with the game it is then possible for the teacher to motivate a very valuable discussion, as it allows him/her to draw out analogies with real life, e.g. what school goals (or 'treasure') would we like to achieve and what prevents us from achieving these. Children mention things like wishing to 'learn more', 'be better at spelling', 'have more friends'. They are then encouraged to look at the obstacles that occur within the group or themselves that prevent them from achieving these goals. They mention aspects like 'other kids talking', 'me not listening', 'I spoil others' games'. The class and the child concerned then brainstorm ideas to help those self-selected children overcome their obstacles in order that they can reach their chosen target. Children can then make individual 'action-plans' that will involve agreements from themselves or others to change certain behaviours in order that their chosen 'treasure' can be reached.

Observation   It is an extremely co-operative game as it demands that in order to support the treasure-seeker's quest the other children have to create a 'pin-dropping' silence. This quality of silence is always reached by every class group because of their absorption in and enjoyment of the game. It is therefore possible, at a different time, to discuss with the children the importance and quality of certain silences. More importantly, it encourages children to think clearly about their behaviour as the physical aspects of the game can easily be understood in abstract terms.

Can I be You?

Good for   Empathy.
Expressing feelings without feeling threatened.
Building group trust and support.

What to do   Sitting in a circle, the teacher or the children will identify an emotion to be explored that day, e.g. worry. Anonymously, children complete a written sentence such as 'I am worried that some of the big boys will trip me up at lunchtime' on a slip of paper. All the papers are then placed in a central container and the children take it in turns to remove a paper from the container, read it, then take a turn to talk about it to the group as if the reader were the writer of that sentence.

Development   Other children often wish to expand on certain speakers' topics. This they may do when the speaker has stopped talking. They can get up, go over to the speaker, stand behind him/her. place a hand on the shoulder and carry on speaking – still as if it were their own topic and talking in the first person singular, e.g. 'Sometimes when I come to school my stomach gets all swirly when I think of big kids teasing me.' The teacher can then ask the group to choose certain of the worries they would like to deal with and as a group suggest ideas to help alleviate those particular problems. At no time is any pressure placed on any child to 'own' the worry.

Observation   This activity helps timid or wary children who would like to talk about their dilemmas and think of solutions but aren't ready to 'risk' themselves publicly.

I think it is to here everybodys veins on something.

Examples from *Turn Your School Round* (1993)

Send a Ripple

Good for   Helping concentration.

What to do   In a circle, the teacher explains that he/she is the rain, denoted by waving the fingers. Participants must pass the action on around the circle. The teacher is then thunder and mimes this by slapping his/her knees. Again the action is passed around the circle. The teacher then alternates rain and thunder movement *until* the next movement reaches his/her place in the circle. Finally the teacher 'brings out the sun' by folding arms, and this action is also passed around the circle.

Discussion   What helped us know the correct movement to make? Why is concentration important in your school work?

Smile or Frown

Good for Helping children to make their feelings explicit and become more reflective. Provides useful information and different perspectives for the teacher.

What to do In a circle, each child says what they did or did not enjoy about that day, or teaching session. Sentences to complete can include:

'I enjoyed ...'
'I did not like ...'
'It was nice when ...'

Try to end with positive statements.

Discussion How could the children and teacher improve teaching sessions?

Getting to Know You

Good for Improving listening and talking skills, self-awareness and self-disclosure.

What to do In small groups, children get into pairs with the person sitting next to them, one child is A and one B. A becomes the interviewer and questions B to find out as much about him/her as possible. A then reports back to the group as much as can be recalled about B. The process is then reversed.

Development Children can draw up a list of questions beforehand. Each child makes a Booster Poster about their partner, with positive statements.

Discussion What interesting new things did you discover about your partner?

Copy the Leader

Good for Developing concentration and eye contact, and having fun

What to do In a circle, a leader begins a movement that is copied by all the circle. The leader then provides a new movement, which is again copied.

Development One player is the 'detective' and stands outside the circle (not looking) while a new leader is chosen. Once the action is in progress, the detective must come into the middle of the circle and try to identify the leader.

Discussion What helps us to be accurate in copying the movement? When and why is concentration important in school?

Give a Good Wish

Good for Encouraging children to think about the needs and wishes of others.

What to do In pairs (but not close friends together) children write or draw a wish for their partners, thinking of something they might really like. It need not be an object:: e.g. 'I wish you could be an astronaut and fly to the moon.' The wishes are then exchanged, read and discussed.

Development All children hang up a stocking with their names on. On separate pieces of paper, each child must write down a positive statement about the five children sitting to his/her right, and put the statements into the correct stockings. Everyone can then read what has been written about them.

Discussion What sorts of thing, other than objects, make people happy? What nice 'ideals' could we wish for (kindness, gentleness, consideration etc)?

I think circle time is for thanking people, saying sorry to people and helping people to solve thier problems.

Who Has Gone?

Good for Developing group awareness, questioning techniques and observation.

What to do In a circle, the children sit with eyes closed or blindfolded and not touching each other. A chosen child touches another, who quietly leaves the circle. The remainder, still with eyes blindfolded, are allowed to ask the first child a set number of questions (excluding names), e.g. three, before attempting to guess the identity of the missing child. If the guess is incorrect, a further question session follows.

Development In pairs, children study the appearance of their partners, then turn back to back and slightly alter their appearance, e.g. push up sleeve, roll down sock, unbutton cardigan. They then face each other again and try to guess what change has been made.

Discussion What helped us think of good questions? Discuss observation and the idea of specific and useful questions.

Zoom and Eek

Good for   Developing awareness of the importance of 'sharing together'.

What to do   In a circle, one child starts a 'car' going round the circle by saying 'zoom' and turning his/her head quickly to the next person on the right. The next person repeats this action and it continues around the circle until a child says 'eek'. The car then changes direction and the 'zoom' sound goes the other way until the next 'eek'. At first the teacher can say 'zoom' and 'eek' and then the children can determine the car's movements themselves. Some children can be selfish in their use of the 'eek' and can confine the action to only one part of the circle. This then needs to be highlighted.

Discussion   How can we be considerate and ensure that all participants share in the action and enjoyment? How can we be more considerate of other people's feelings in general?

If I Were ...

Good for   Developing self-awareness, enhancing speaking skills, helping the expression of feelings in a safe situation.

What to do   In a circle, each participant finishes a statement such as 'If I were a bird I would want to be a ... because ...'

Development Use other categories, e.g. famous people, animals, colours. Activity can be done in small groups or pairs within the circle. Ideas can be written down and used in drama or art.

Discussion   What can my choice tell me about myself?

Example of a themed Circle Time session from *Quality Circle Time in the Primary Classroom* (1996). The theme is Kindness.

Activity 1 – Fruit Salad

Aim To mix up the children so they are not sitting by friends.

What to do Versions of this game are described on pages 15 and 18.

Activity 2 – Kind comments

Aim To introduce the idea of making positive statements about others so that they feel good.

What to do Each child forms a pair with the child sitting directly to his right. The members of each pair question one another so that they can each give three positive statements about their partner, e.g.

'John is good at football. He can run really fast. He helps his dad with the garden.'

'Vicky has lovely soft hair. She is always polite. She helps at the riding school.'

Activity 3 – Something kind

Aim To focus the children's attention on kind acts.

What to do The children sit in an inward-facing circle. Using the conch, each child completes the sentence: 'Something kind I did was ...'

Open forum The teacher asks the children to consider how they felt when someone was kind or unkind to them. He/she then asks how they felt when they were kind or unkind themselves and encourages the responses that everyone benefits from kindness, but no one benefits from unkindness. Does any child have a problem with someone being unkind to them that they would like help with? Don't forget the ground rule that a child must not name another child in a negative way, but must say 'someone' or 'some people'.

Activity 4 – Musical statues with mime

Aim Fun, ending game.

What to do All the children stand in a circle. The teacher gives them a task they must mime – e.g. washing a car, hanging clothes on a washing line – while music is played. When the music stops they must freeze. Anyone who moves is out and sits down.

'A special person'

Resources	Two animal glove puppets (Salt and Pepper). A mirror inside a box, small enough to be easily passed around a circle of children.

Script

Pepper	Hello, Salt. You don't look very happy today. Is anything wrong?
Salt	I'm fed up because I'm not really good at anything. Danny is really good at running and Parvi is good at reading. Rachel can do all her maths and James is the best at football. Everyone seems to be good at something except for me. I feel so ordinary and a nobody.
Pepper	Well, Salt. I've got a box here and if you look inside you will see someone who is really special. Would you like to have a look?
Salt	I suppose so.
Pepper	But you must keep quiet and not say who the special person is yet.
	Salt looks in the box and says 'Oh!' in surprise.
Pepper	Children, would you like to look in my box and see who the special person is? You must keep very quiet and not say anything until everyone has had a look.
	The children pass the box around the circle and look at the reflection of themselves in the mirror.
Pepper	Now, children, you have all had a look at the special person inside my box. Who was it?
	Pause.
Pepper	Yes, it was you. All of you are special. I'm special and, Salt, you are special.
Salt	But how can I be special when I am not good at anything?
Pepper	Everyone is good at something, Salt. You are good at being kind and helpful. You're good at looking after your pet hamster and you're good at telling jokes.
Salt	Yes, I suppose I am. I didn't think about those things. They didn't seem important.
Pepper	Everything we are good at is important to someone or in some way.

Salt	I feel so much better now, Pepper. I don't feel I'm not important any more.
	Salt turns to the children.
Salt	Let's all say together, 'I am special'.
	The children repeat this several times.
Development	The children complete a round of 'I am good at ...'. It is important to stress that they may choose something at school or at home so that everyone can find some skill to celebrate. Make sure that no derogatory comments are made in response to any child's statement.

Checklist of Quality Circle Time techniques and approaches

Games

They unite the class, are enjoyable and break down tensions. They exert their own discipline and encourage self-control and group participation. They encourage verbal and physical contact. Many can be adapted to help children think about abstract concepts (e.g. trust and co-operation, achievement).

Rounds

A theme or idea is selected and everyone takes a turn to speak; sometimes a sentence can be started and each child completes it, (e.g. 'I feel happy when ...'). Every comment is acceptable an no one may comment on what anyone else says. Anyone can say 'Pass'.

Brainstorming

Ask for as many ideas as fast as possible without prioritising them; this emphasises corporate creativity and that everyone has a valid and valuable contribution to make. Later, consult the group to structure ideas into categories and use as a basis for decision-making.

Drama approach

This helps pupils to actively engage in what makes sense to them in terms of past experience and present levels of understanding. Role-play reflects a true valuing of the individual, precisely because the 'dynamic' is the individual. Drama enables students to express hidden feelings, discuss problems, practise empathy, try out new behaviour, portray generalised social problems and the dynamics of group interaction, and emphasises the importance of non-verbal emotional response. Drama is an effective diagnostic tool and changes attitudes.

Discussion

Discussion requires the putting forward of more than one point of view. It is essentially a 'give and take' activity of a highly reciprocal nature. Discussion requires those engaged to be prepared to examine and be responsive to the different opinions put forward.

Reflection

A deliberate co-operative task which encourages the group to reflect on the meanings underlying the experience they've just shared. It is a group negotiation for meaning, an attempt to expand the current spheres of reference to a wider understanding of the meanings involved.

National articles written by Jenny Mosley and others about her self-esteem work with primary and secondary schoolchildren

Jones, J., 'Circulating the secrets of good discipline' *The Independent* Education Section, 9 May 1991

Kirkman, S., 'Ring of Confidence', *Times Educational Supplement*, 12 October 1990

Lang, P. & Mosley, J., 'Promoting positive outcomes in schools through self-esteem and circle time', 1992

Mosley J., 'Dramatherapy in education enhances self-concept', *Journal of Educational Therapy* vol. 1 no. 4, 1987

Mosley J., 'Drama with children experiencing adjustment problems', *Dramatherapy: Journal of the British Association of Dramatherapists*, 1988

Mosley J., 'Dramatherapy: helping children with behaviour problems', *Maladjustment and Therapeutic Education* vol. 6 no. 2, 1988

Mosley, J., 'Some implications arising from a small-scale study of a circle-based programme initiated for the tutorial period', *Pastoral Care in Education* vol. 6 no. 2, 1988

Mosley J., 'A circular response to the Elton Report', *Maladjustment and Therapeutic Education* vol. 9 no. 3, 1991

Mosley J. 'A circular response to the Elton Report: a social context for improving behaviour', *British Psychological Society Education Review Section*, vol. 15 no. 2, 1991

Mosley, J., 'Building self-esteem in the primary school', *Home and School: a magazine for parents and teachers*, October 1991

Mosley, J., 'An evaluative account of the working of a dramatherapy peer support group in a comprehensive school', *Support for Learning: Journal of the National Association of Remedial Education*, vol.6 no.4, 1991

Mosley, J., 'Developing a whole school approach to circle time', *Primary Life* vol. 1:3, Autumn 1992

Mosley, J., 'Is there a place for counselling in schools', *Counselling: Journal for the British Association of Counselling*, vol.4 no.2, 1993

Mosley, J., 'Value Added PACTs' (how Wiltshire teachers are helping to raise the self-esteem of children and adults in primary schools), *Special Children* no. 55, March 1992

Mosley J., 'A whole school approach to self-esteem and positive behaviour', *Topic* (NFER) no. 9, Spring 1993

Mosley J. & Flynn, F., 'The management of pupil behaviour', *BBC Teaching Today* booklet, 1992

Shaw, K., 'Developing peer support groups: a practical INSET response to the Elton Report', *Pastoral Care in Education*, October 1991

Training and Resources

Training for your staff

The Jenny Mosley Consultancies can provide well-trained consultants, experienced in all aspects of the Whole School Quality Circle Time Model, who will visit your school to run courses and workshops for teachers and support staff. Try our key introductory course for primary and secondary schools on the **Whole School Quality Circle Time Model**:

- On a Closure (INSET) day, all staff, teachers, lunchtime supervisors, ancillary and administration staff are invited to participate in a day that focuses on all aspects of the model, including team-building, developing positive ethos and valuing individuals.

- On a Working In School day, the school does not close and the Quality Circle Time approach is demonstrated with whole groups of pupils observed by a range of staff. In addition, Circle Time meetings can be held for lunchtime supervisors and an action plan for the school is drawn up with key members of staff.

- The Top Value Option (discounted price) is to book both the above plus a follow-up day for evaluation and advice.

Other courses for schools

The following are examples of courses offered by our team of highly qualified and experienced consultants, available in similar format to the above:

> Happier Lunchtimes
> Assessing the effectiveness of your self-esteem, anti-bullying and positive
>   behaviour policies
> Developing peer mediation
> Developing PSHE, citizenship and emotional literacy policies through
>   Quality Circle Time
> Re-energising your circle time policies with *Quality* ideas
> Children beyond – what more can we do?
> Involving everyone in Quality Circle Time

Accredited, specialist trainers only!

Our research and experience reveal that the Whole School Quality Circle Time Model can become diluted or vulnerable when people who have never attended one of our in-depth courses offer training based on our model. Jenny Mosley holds week long in-depth courses nationally and then awards accompanying certificates.

For details of all the above, contact the Project Manager by any of the means listed on page 42. A list of accredited trainers is available.

Books and other resources

Turn Your School Round by Jenny Mosley
Comprehensive management manual for the whole school community to develop positive relationships through circle time. (LDA)

Quality Circle Time by Jenny Mosley
Essential guide to enhancing self-esteem and self-discipline, for teachers wishing to put the Whole School Circle Time model into their classrooms, with hundreds of ideas and lesson plans. (LDA)

More Quality Circle Time by Jenny Mosley
Develops the application of the model in a sequel to the above. Includes ten-minute circle times for nursery children to practice specific skills. (LDA)

Here We Go Round by Jenny Mosley & Helen Sonnet
Delightfully illustrated book of Quality Circle Time activity plans for the Early Years in response to the QCA guidance document, with sessions for each of the six areas of learning. (Positive Press)

Photocopiable Materials for use with the Jenny Mosley Circle Time Model by Jenny Mosley
Charts, target sheets, achievement ladders, awards, congratulations cards, invitations and much more. (Positive Press)

Circle Time ed. Jenny Mosley
User-friendly low-budget, high-value booklet, with excellent lesson plans for reception, KS1 and KS2. (Positive Press)

The Circle Book by Jenny Mosley
Inspiring collection of responses to Quality Circle Time, with feedback from teachers and children and great suggestions for games and activities. (Positive Press)

Working Towards a Whole School Policy on Self-Esteem and Positive Behaviour by Jenny Mosley
How to write and operate an effective policy involving teachers, children, parents, MDSAs – everyone! With background information and ideas based on schools' experience using the Quality Circle Time model. (Positive Press)

Bridging the Circle: Transition through Quality Circle Time by Anne Cowling and Penny Vine
Thoughtful and effective Circle Time lesson plans for years 6 and 7 supporting the often intimidating transition from primary to secondary school. With photocopiable resources.

All Round Success by Jenny Mosley
Simply set-out practical ideas and games to help children with their social skills. (WEST)

Coming Round Again by Jenny Mosley
Sequel to the above, outlining how to pull together a range of fun activities into a themed approach. (WEST)

Guidelines for Primary Midday Supervisors by Jenny Mosley
A friendly, practical self-help booklet to be given directly to lunchtime supervisors as part of the policy to boost their skills and self-esteem. (WEST)

Create Happier Lunchtimes by Jenny Mosley
Sequel to the above, offering extra ideas and both indoor and outdoor games

Assemblies to Teach Golden Rules by Margaret Goldthorpe and Lucy Nutt
Dynamic and fun assemblies for developing the moral values behind Golden Rules, based on positive reward for good behaviour rather than punishment for negative actions. (LDA)

Poems for Circle Time & Literacy Hour by Margaret Goldthorpe
Poems of simplicity and fun, to help children look at serious issues in a relaxed way within our five-step model. (LDA)

Effective IEPs through Circle Time by Margaret Goldthorpe
Practical solutions to writing Individual Education Plans for children with emotional and behavioural difficulties, using Quality Circle Time. (LDA)

We also have books on Quality Circle Time for secondary schools, and on adult subjects such as assertiveness and self-esteem.

Titles in preparation (Positive Press and LDA):

> **All Year Round** – exciting ideas for peaceful playtimes
> **Stepping Stones to Success** – a planned journey through the foundation stage
> **Ring of Confidence** – personal safety for the foundation stage
> **101 Games for Self-Esteem**
> **Golden Moments for Busy Teachers**

Training video: Quality Circle Time in Action
An excellent in-depth resource for staff training, showing Jenny demonstrating her model with KS1 and KS2 pupils. Includes booklet with her five steps to Quality Circle Time. (LDA)

Jenny Mosley's Self-Esteem Builders Set
Contains motivational stickers for congratulating children on moral values and circle time skills; two colourful themed class target sheets with reusable stickers to mark positive behaviour towards a particular target; reward certificates for achievements such as deciding to improve; responsibility badges for boosting children's self-esteem through special tasks such as being special child of the week; and a golden rules poster set for classroom and playground. **Items also available separately**. (LDA)

Jenny Mosley's Quality Circle Time Kitbag
To keep circle times exciting and fresh: contains two puppets, blindfold, cloak, rainstick, teddy, treasure chest, cassette tape and booklet of lesson ideas. **Rainstick** also available separately.

Playground Friends Hats and Baseball Cap
Brightly coloured incentives to support your whole school lunchtime policy and help pupils take the special job of playground helper seriously.

Golden Moment Mug
Eye-catching blue and gold mug to help you recharge your energy in that precious break from the demands of teaching.

Painted 'Talking' Egg
Every design of these handpainted lacquered eggs is unique. Holding the egg means it's that child's chance to speak while everyone else listens.

New lines being introduced:

    Friendship stops for the playground
    Finger and glove puppets
    Parachute
    Sandtimers
    Rainbow Song pack

Contact details for Jenny Mosley Consultancies / Positive Press Ltd:

28A Gloucester Road, Trowbridge,
Wiltshire, BA14 0AA, England

Tel. 01225 719204 (books and products)

Tel. 01225 767157 (training)

Fax 01225 755631

E-mail: circletime@jennymosley.demon.co.uk

Website: www.jennymosley.demon.co.uk